MW00329310

Healing

HEARTBREAK
JOURNAL

—✠—

Love After Heartbreak, Vol. I
COMPANION BOOK

STEPHAN LABOSSIERE

@stephanspeaks

Healing Heartbreak Journal
Love After Heartbreak, Vol. 1 Companion Book

Copyright ©2019 by Stephan Labossiere for Stephan Speaks, LLC

Published by Highly Favored Publishing

First Edition: July 2019

All rights reserved. No part of this book may be used or reproduced in any manner whatsoever without written permission except in the case of brief quotations embodied in critical articles or reviews.

For information, contact Highly Favored Publishing – highlyfavoredent@gmail.com

Unless otherwise indicated, all Scripture quotations are taken from the Holy Bible, New Living Translation, copyright © 1996, 2004, 2015 by Tyndale House Foundation. Used by permission of Tyndale House Publishers, Inc., Carol Stream, Illinois 60188. All rights reserved.

Scripture quotations marked (NIV) are taken from the Holy Bible, New International Version®, NIV®. Copyright © 1973, 1978, 1984, 2011 by Biblica, Inc.™ Used by permission of Zondervan. All rights reserved worldwide. www.zondervan.com The "NIV" and "New International Version" are trademarks registered in the United States Patent and Trademark Office by Biblica, Inc.™

Editor & Creative Consultant: C. Nzingha Smith

Formatting: Ya Ya Ya Creative – www.yayayacreative.com

ISBN No. 978-0-9980189-5-9

PRINTED AND BOUND IN THE UNITED STATES OF AMERICA

Table of Contents

"He heals the brokenhearted and binds up their wounds."
–Psalm 147:3, NLT

Introduction

The *Healing Heartbreak Journal* is a companion book for *Love After Heartbreak, Vol. I*. Its purpose is to give you additional resources on your self-healing journey. As I explained in *Love After Heartbreak, Vol. I*, everyone is in a different place within the pain spectrum. For this reason, results with my healing process will vary.

The effort you put in toward completing all the exercises in this journal are critical to getting the results you truly desire. This companion book is meant to help you dive deeper into self-discovery, which is the only true beginning point for manifesting your dream life and relationship.

As long as you continue to focus on external things and not do your part to change the one thing you actually have control over, you, it will be difficult, if not impossible for you to experience success in your relationships. You're in control here. Take this time to work on you. To learn you. To accept you. To learn how to love you. When you do all these things, you'll be ready for unlimited possibilities in your relationships.

As always, be open to the information I'm going to share with you. Be willing to do your part. Believe you'll be able to reap the many benefits awaiting you at the end of this journey and it will be possible for you.

As you prepare to dive deeper into your self-healing journey, I want to encourage you that "it is well." This is a statement of faith I want you to begin declaring over your life. It has nothing to do with your current circumstances, financial situation, job status, what you've experienced throughout your life, the hurts you're working to get over, past disappointments, injustices you've seen on the news, or anything else.

Everything is subject to change for the better. You have to know and believe when you're going through that "it is well." Take a moment and read 2 Kings, chapter four and be encouraged in your faith. There are few things we have control over in life. Our thoughts or perspective is one. What we choose to believe is another. What do you believe and who do you believe? Your answer to these two questions will ultimately determine your outcomes in life.

The Shunamite woman in 2 Kings believed that "it was well" despite the fact that her son died in her lap and lay dead on the prophet's couch. However, despite what her eyes saw, she got exactly what she believed for. She refused to believe anything other than the outcome she wanted to see happen. Her unwavering faith, not her circumstances, determined her results. It turned out well with her and those connected to her.

It's important for you to raise your level of expectation of who God is. Believe God for your healing now, in advance, and it will be possible. I pray that as you continue on your journey toward self-healing, you'll develop a conviction in your spirit about experiencing complete healing. I also pray you'll have a concrete belief in the God we serve. Choose to create this reality in your life no matter what. Decide every day that your report and your testimony will be: "it is well."

> *"What do you mean, 'If I can'?" Jesus asked.*
> *"Anything is possible if a person believes."*
> –Mark 9:23, NLT

Opening Prayer

Pray this prayer with me:

Heavenly Father, I pray a release of your supernatural comfort, peace, and grace upon everyone reading this book right now. I pray that you would cleanse us with your healing power and love. Rid us of all the memories from hurt, pain, and disappointment we've endured, which were necessary for our growth and promotion.

God, grant us the gift of compassion so we may handle others with care because we are all sensitive and in need of encouragement and peace. I also pray that you give us clarity of mind. Open up our eyes of understanding so that we may master the lessons needed to receive, pursue, and recover everything meant for us.

Thank you, God, for renewed faith and courage to do what it takes to be our best selves as you've purposed us to be. We're making the choice to live our lives more abundantly.

We're making the decision to co-create the lives we want to live now and going forward according to your will. Your word says, when two or more are gathered together in your name that you are with them. Thank you for your presence as we continue our collective healing journeys. By faith, we declare it done and so. Amen.

belief

Poet C. Nzingha Smith

Seeing my smile
wide   bright
it's not me being fake
I'm exercising,
the muscles in my face—works—mix with faith,
permit smiling in spite of the pain,
medicine to help cure what aches
being sure of what I have the courage to create
certain of what I cannot see or feel, yet
knowing, one day
I'll actually possess—evidence—the intangible,
attracted to my decision to put forth that genuine smile,
a choice, powerful enough
to alter my future realities, activating healing within me,
growth, both journey and destination,
not beyond my control
nor predicated on anyone other than,
I, decide, daily
until reached, I'm practicing
interacting with the future,
healed me, now
accepting the grace sufficient for my today,
helps me go on
demonstrating—despite what I face—my belief.

How Not to
Get Over Heartbreak

In *Love After Heartbreak, Vol. I*, I identified several things you shouldn't do to get over your heartbreak. They include:

- Getting Under Someone to Get Over Someone

- Suppressing Your Feelings

- Using Distractions to Cope

- Only Praying About It

- Waiting for Time to Heal You

However, I also realize it's possible you've already taken matters into your own hands or listened to the ill-advice of someone who might be dwelling in their own past hurts. If this is the case, you might need to identify or come to terms with ways you're used to handling your hurt, pain, and disappointments. These habits have probably now become natural behavior for you.

The following exercise is going to help you identify your natural behaviors when it comes to processing your hurtful experiences.

Remember, behavior is learned. Once we develop habits both positive and negative, we tend to do them without needing to think about them. However, we can also unlearn negative behavior patterns and replace them with positive ones to help improve our lives.

Exercise: IDENTIFYING YOUR CURRENT WAYS OF COPING WITH HEARTBREAK

Write down the methods you've used to get over heartbreak and hurt.

_____

_____

_____

_____

_____

_____

_____

_____

_____

_____

_____

_____

When you have yet to truly learn and embrace who you really are, being alone is like spending time with a stranger and that can be scary.

How did each method make you feel? Better or Worse? Why?

You're so much more than how you see yourself.

Did you experience any side-effects from your choices? These can be both negative and positive.

_____

_____

_____

_____

_____

_____

_____

_____

_____

_____

_____

You have the power to co-create your entire life
—including your love life— through your choices.

How Early Experiences with Heartbreak Shape Us

We're all shaped by our early experiences. This is especially true when it comes to our early experiences with heartbreak. It could be something we experienced personally, or it can be an experience we witnessed someone close to us go through, similar to the story I shared about my father's affair.

As I mentioned in *Love After Heartbreak, Vol. I*, the damage my father's affair caused lingered within me and negatively altered my outlook on love and relationships. I honestly didn't know how devastating this experience would ultimately become for me. Even though I was outside of my mother's hurt, it shaped my early perception of love, relationships, and commitment, entirely. While I was sympathizing with my mother's pain, I didn't notice my own painful scars beginning to form from the experience.

Much later in my life, I had to face the fact that witnessing my mother's hurt, created a negative perspective of relationships for me. This negative perception fed all my early relationships with a toxic fire that burned them alive, one after the other. From my mother's experience, I developed a true fear of hurting people. Out of this fear came a hypersensitivity toward other people and an obsession with not wanting to cheat on women.

However, I allowed this fear to grow out of control. It kept me from exploring potential relationships with women I genuinely cared for and that might have had the potential to grow into sustainable, loving relationships. Operating from this extreme place of fear kept me guarded, frustrated, and angry. It kept me in a negative mindset and it ultimately kept love away. I paid a very high price for not wanting to acknowledge or deal with my pain and hurt from this early experience.

It wasn't until I dealt with the root issues connected to this early experience with hurt, pain, and heartbreak that I was able to heal properly and move past the negative behaviors I'd developed in my adult life.

Take some time now and think back to your childhood and early adolescent experiences. Think about your parents, siblings, friends, and any other people who might have had an influence on you as a child. Pay attention to whether or not the memories that surface for you create warm feelings or negative feelings within you. Also pay attention to how your body responds to the answers to the following questions.

Exercise: EXPLORING YOUR EARLY EXPERIENCES

What emotions come to mind when you think back to your earlier relationships? Family, friends, crushes.

_____

_____

_____

_____

_____

Did you experience or witness other people's pain and hurt as a child? If so, what thought patterns developed for you from them?

_____

_____

_____

_____

_____

Did you develop any fears around love, relationships, and marriage as a result of these early experiences? If so, what are they?

_____

_____

_____

_____

_____

_____

It's important to do the work now and get to the root cause of your deeply held feelings and beliefs. It's important for us as a culture and society to stop just treating the symptoms.

Our beliefs fuel the stories we play in our minds, which we eventually live out in our daily lives.

Again, they could be from things you had to go through or from your having to witness other people's experiences. We normally internalize other people's pain without even realizing it. When we do this, the result is a deeply felt fear we record in our minds based off how we felt in the moment, even if we forget about it the next minute. This fear is stored in our subconscious mind. Once the fear is stored subconsciously, our body and emotions react to environmental triggers stemming from the original, recorded fear. This causes us to act out in some way as a defense toward the perceived fear. We do this over and over again throughout our lives without ever really putting much thought into why.

Until now.

Let's spend some time working through identifying your experiences and the feelings and beliefs you associate with them.

Unfortunately, a lot of people don't receive a healthy foundation when it comes to:

- How to love and accept themselves unconditionally.

- How to give and receive love in relationships.

- How to handle and express their positive and negative emotions.

- How to communicate their wants and needs in a healthy way where they feel heard and valued.

- Witnessing healthy, balanced, successful relationships.

From a foundational standpoint, in order to move to a healthier place in your adult life, it will take you being intentional about unlearning what you know and replacing it with what might actually work for you now.

Just because it's what you saw or were used to growing up, doesn't mean you need to continue the behavior as an adult. Especially, if the behavior isn't serving you and your relationships now.

You have a choice. Do what actually works for you or at least try to figure it out. The reality is you might not know. You might have only been shown what not to do in relationships. You might only know negative outcomes that you don't want to keep experiencing.

Guess what? Either way, it's okay. It's a starting point. We all have to start from somewhere.

Going forward, you have the power to change whatever it is that doesn't add happiness and joy to your life. However, you must be willing to give up the belief that other people can make you happy. It's simply not true. Other people can only add to a foundation of happiness you must create for yourself.

No matter what, you always have the power to choose.

Exercise: MY EARLY EXPERIENCES WITH LOVE

What were your early childhood and adolescent examples of love?

_____

_____

_____

_____

_____

Did you grow up in a loving family environment? If not, what was it like?

_____

_____

_____

_____

_____

Did you feel loved and supported as a child? Did the people closest to you make you feel worthy of receiving their love? Why or Why Not?

_____

_____

_____

_____

_____

How did the people around you show you and each other affection?

_____

_____

_____

_____

_____

You are free to decide that you deserve better...
but only you can decide.

Do you find yourself practicing some of the same love habits you learned as a child in your adult life? What are they? Be as specific as possible.

You are growing and healing every day. Be patient with yourself and the process.

_____

_____

_____

_____

_____

_____

_____

_____

_____

_____

_____

_____

_____

Do these behaviors serve you now? Do they create happiness in and for you and your relationships? If not, why do you still practice them?

_____

_____

_____

_____

_____

_____

_____

"For we are God's Masterpiece."
–Ephesians 2:10, NLT

_____

_____

_____

_____

_____

_____

What type of behaviors have you observed from others that you actually like, and think would better serve you? Can you begin practicing them?

_____

_____

_____

_____

_____

_____

_____

_____

_____

There is nothing in life more powerful than love.

_____

_____

_____

Allow love to flow freely from your heart and watch how quickly and abundantly you receive love in return.

Learning Your
Love Language(s)

According to Dr. Gary Chapman there are five main love languages.

- *Acts of Service*- practical things you do to show your partner love.

- *Words of Affirmation*- saying loving, kind words to your partner.

- *Quality Time*- taking time to experience things together.

- *Receiving Gifts*- a tangible item you receive that expresses love.

- *Physical Touch*- physical touch that communicates love.

"The object of love is not getting something you want but doing something for the well-being of the one you love," writes Gary Chapman in *The 5 Love Languages: The Secret to Love That Lasts*. "It is a fact, however, that when we receive affirming words, we are far more likely to be motivated to reciprocate."

Do you know your love language(s)? What are they? If not, spend some time thinking about the things that make you feel loved by others consistently. Write them down.

_____

_____

_____

_____

_____

_____

_____

_____

_____

_____

_____

_____

Do the ways you need to receive love match up with the ways you're experiencing love in your relationships? Why or why not?

_____

*Always know
the difference
between what you're
getting, and
what you deserve.*

_____

_____

_____

_____

_____

_____

_____

_____

_____

_____

_____

How do you communicate your needs & wants in relationships? Are these ways effective? Do they produce the results you want?

_____

_____

_____

_____

_____

_____

_____

_____

_____

Sometimes you have to put aside what you feel for them, and pay attention to what their actions are saying they feel for you.

_____

_____

_____

_____

Check-in Time: PERSONAL REFLECTION

Use the next few pages to take time to reflect on the things that we've covered in this section and what you've discovered about yourself and your experiences so far. How are you feeling? What can you do to reward yourself for your courage and commitment to your healing? Do it!

_____

_____

_____

_____

_____

_____

Smile beautiful. It helps to relieve stress, elevate your mood, keep you looking younger, and attract more things for you to smile about.

_____

_____

_____

_____

_____

AFFIRMATION: I am at peace in every area of my life.

_____

_____

_____

_____

_____

_____

_____

_____

_____

_____

_____

_____

Prioritize YOU. Be happy in real life.
Make your well-being, your priority.

AFFIRMATION: I am learning how to accept myself.

_____

_____

_____

_____

*You are deserving
of everything good
in life. Believe you
will receive it.*

_____

_____

_____

_____

_____

_____

_____

_____

PART I

UNDERSTANDING

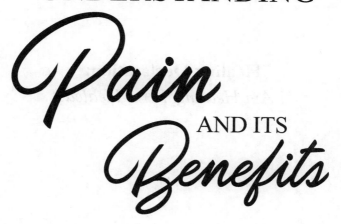

Pain

AND ITS

Benefits

Healing Declaration:
"I Am Healing. I Am Healed."

The Truth About Being Hurt

It's so important for you to remember that this time of working through your heartbreak and healing is a reset period for your life.

Pain and hurt are teachers. The lessons they teach, even though uncomfortable, are lessons we need to be willing to accept. The lessons help make us better people. They build our character, confidence, and help us to be better prepared for the trials of life we have yet to face.

Being prepared and being paranoid are not the same things.

It's important to know that you don't need to run from pain. Running from hurt and disappointment doesn't teach you how to deal with it. Every time hurt or pain comes your way, it gives you an opportunity to learn and grow. Being mindful of this allows you to begin to see and understand the lessons each experience you go through is supposed to teach you.

The ultimate lesson I want you to learn is that you always have a choice. You can choose to stay down and hurt, or you can decide to take the necessary steps to recover. You can get back up again. You have the ability, whether you realize it or not, to overcome any pain thrown your way. It all starts with you making the decision to get back up again.

A good strategy for you to use when you experience pain, hurt, and disappointments is to figure out how to best process through your emotions as you're experiencing them.

Remember, never suppress how you feel. Instead, come up with healthy and productive ways to work through your feelings and to release them. Doing so will ensure they don't keep you stuck and hinder your forward progress. There are both negative and positive ways to process through your emotions.

NEGATIVE BEHAVIORS	POSITIVE ALTERNATIVES
• Blowing up on people	• Take time alone to cool down
• Using drugs or sex to cope	• Go for a walk/run to release anger
• Harming yourself or others	• Take time to pray
• Verbally abusing yourself/others	• Talk to a counselor/coach
• Isolating yourself for long periods	• Reach out to others for support

Most people's habits of dealing with their emotions stem from how they learned to express themselves as children. It may sound crazy but think about how you act now compared to the younger version of yourself. Chances are if you threw temper tantrums as a child, you're likely to still express negative emotions in the same way now, or if you were withdrawn, the same applies. You'll be able to explore this more in the next exercise.

Exercise: IDENTIFYING YOUR CURRENT EMOTIONAL PROCESS

How did you cope with disappointments as a child? Did you fall out? Kick things around? Punch the wall? Lock yourself in the closet? Pick a fight with your sibling? How do you normally handle your emotions now? Are your methods helpful & healthy for you? Remember this is a non-judgement zone. You're here to observe, not judge or criticize yourself.

_____

_____

_____

_____

You can't change what you don't face.

_____

_____

_____

_____

_____

_____

Surrender to what is. Let go of what was.

Look over your list. Think about more healthy alternatives you can do to replace any of the current unhealthy behaviors. Below rewrite your current unhealthy behaviors and the positive alternatives next to or after them. Think about how the positive alternatives might make you feel.

Where there is love, there is life.

Follow your heart but take your brain with you.

Now that you have positive alternatives to choose from when processing through your emotions, I want you to make a list of things that comfort you. It could be a favorite food, place, person, song, etc. What are things that help make you feel better when you are going through?

_____

_____

_____

Not all storms come to disrupt your life, some come to clear your path.

_____

_____

_____

_____

_____

_____

_____

_____

You are love. Choose to love and approve of yourself as you are.

Match up your new healthy alternative behaviors with the things that make you feel good. This is a good starting point for creating your personal grieving process. Use the space below to brainstorm some ideas before laying it all out day by day.

_____

_____

_____

_____

_____

_____   *There is no*
                                      remedy for love
_____   *but to love*
                                      more.

_____

_____

_____

_____

_____

Do what makes you happy. Be with who makes you smile.
Laugh as much as you breathe. Love as long as you live.

I shared with you what my grieving process looks like in *Vol. I* of *Love After Heartbreak*. Take a moment and review pages 45-51.

Under normal circumstances, I usually give myself three full days to process my emotions and take time to grieve from the disappointing and hurtful experiences that I endure. I believe in honoring myself and my feelings in this process. Just because I'm a man, I don't need to pretend that things that happen in my life don't affect me or can't hurt me. This simply isn't true.

However, I also know the importance of giving myself a limited number of days for my grieving process so that I don't wallow too long and get stagnant in negative and low energy. I know what works for me and the sooner I process through my negative emotions, the better.

Now you're going to create your own grieving process. You need to figure out the best time frame for you to positively process through your emotions and continue to move forward after future hurtful experiences.

Creating your own grieving process will ensure you don't stay stuck in any negativity or unhealthy headspaces when you face future hurt. You'll get the release you need and can move forward quickly. This will be an invaluable tool to have so you can practice new, healthier habits until they become your new positive behavior default.

Exercise: CREATING YOUR OWN GRIEVING PROCESS

Take time now to map out your grieving process. How many days are you going to give yourself to grieve? What are you going to do each day?

DAY 1: My Grieving Process

_____

_____

_____

_____

_____

_____

God knows when you need more time to prepare for the love and relationship that you truly deserve.

DAY 2: My Grieving Process

_____

_____

_____

_____

DAY 3: My Grieving Process

_____

_____

_____

_____

_____

_____

DAY 4: My Grieving Process

_____

_____

_____

_____

_____

_____

_Self-discovery is the first key to receiving the
love and relationship you desire._

Remember to be honest about what you're feeling and how your experiences effect you. Processing through your emotions is the first step in being able to move forward without allowing those negative feelings to linger. You don't want to suppress them and leave them unresolved.

Give yourself and your emotions the respect they both deserve. It's good to mourn. It's good to grieve. You need it. It's healthy. You need to take time as soon as things happen to process through them and to pay attention to how you feel. Don't wait. The last thing you want to do is suppress things. I want you to stop feeling like you must suppress how you feel about what goes on in your life.

Taking this time to learn how to be honest about how you feel is going to help you bounce back from pain and hurt faster when future issues come up.

No matter what your grieving process looks like, once you get to the last day, it's important for you to begin to participate in the activities that make you feel productive and add to your sense of positive well-being.

By day three or four, depending on how long your grieving process will be, start doing the things you do regularly that make you feel good and bring a smile to your face.

You do this by eating well, drinking plenty of water, and getting enough rest. It takes physical strength to pull yourself back up and keep going. It's easy to keep wallowing in the unhealthy place.

When you're grieving, it's easier to make unhealthy choices because these same choices are probably what you're used to using as a means to cope and deal. So, make sure you decide to actively choose to do better by your last day of grieving.

Once you've decided on what your process will be and the max number of days you think you'll need to go through your normal grieving process, stick to it. Once your grieving period is over, it's done. Wipe the tears and decide to move forward.

Moving forward doesn't mean you won't still have your moments.

Deciding to move forward, simply means you aren't going to consistently dwell in the hurtful, broken place.

Again, no one's expecting you to be perfect with this. However, set a time period and once the time is up, make the decision to move on.

There is real danger in giving yourself too much leeway on your grieving time. You can get to the point that you stay stuck. The one thing I've learned about being hurt is, the longer you wallow and dwell in it, the harder it becomes to get out of that headspace. Believe it or not it's very easy to become comfortable feeling sad and depressed.

Let me be clear here, comfortable doesn't mean you're happy because clearly if you're wallowing in self-pity or sadness, you're not happy.

However, you're no longer going to be that person. You're now better able to handle the down times of life because you've created a blueprint for yourself. You now have a healthier way to process through your emotions.

I want you to begin practicing your new process over and over, until it becomes a natural habit for you, and your natural way of dealing with your emotions going forward.

Check-in Time: PERSONAL REFLECTION

Use the next few pages to take time to reflect on the things that we've covered in this section and what you've discovered about yourself and your experiences so far. How are you feeling? What can you do to reward yourself for your courage and commitment to your healing? Do it!

_____

_____

_____

You are strong.
You are capable.
Everything you need,
you already possess.
You are it.
You are everything.

_____

_____

_____

_____

_____

_____

AFFIRMATION: I am worthy of receiving unconditional love.

_____

_____

_____

_____

_____

_____

_____

_____

_____

_____

_____

_____

_____

_____

The words you speak become the house you live in.

AFFIRMATION: I am enough.

_God approves of you.
Is proud of you.
Thinks the world of you
and is hoping you'll learn
to see yourself the way
He sees you._

Hurt People, Hurt People

Since you're digging deep and doing the work required to heal and make positive changes to better your life, it's important to be clear on what you're working toward. So, how will you know if your work is paying off? You might be wondering, "Am I going to be able to see the changes going on within me in an outward way?" Below are some traits and characteristics of what it looks like to be healthy, whole, and healed.

A healthy, happy person in general will usually exhibit the following types of behaviors. They are:

- Going to be more patient with people.

- Going to see the good in others and actively choose to put their good out in front of them when interacting with others.

- They are calmer and have more peace within themselves to extend to others.

- Going to look for the good in the situation as opposed to the bad.

- Going to side on the side of optimism as opposed to pessimism.

A healthy, happy person in general will usually not exhibit the following types of behaviors. They aren't:

- Going to be so quick to find reasons to be offended by the actions of others.

- Rude and combative, always on the lookout for a fight or altercation of some kind.

- Holding onto a lot of negative energy.

- Going to be so quick to look at life, people, and situations from a negative perspective.

When you're always quick to assume the worst, jump to negative conclusions, or have a negative outlook on situations, this is evidence that there are deeper issues still present within you.

However, when you're not spending your energy fighting, arguing, and exchanging negative energy with others, it allows you to conserve your energy to spend on the things you actually enjoy doing. You'll observe having more peace within you. You'll be able to notice the changes you are making on the inside as you interact with others outwardly.

Again, be patient with yourself. It's not going to be an overnight fix. Everything you've learned up to this point in your life is a result of things you've decided to do over and over again, until it became your habits. You need to allow yourself the same opportunity to develop new, better habits by doing positive, helpful, and healthy actions repeatedly.

Exercise: OBSERVING YOUR TREATMENT OF OTHERS

How do you normally treat the people closest to you? Family, friends, co-workers, romantic partners? Do you speak to them with love & respect?

_____

_____

_____

_____

Boundaries are healthy. NO is a complete sentence and should be a part of your self-care routine.

_____

_____

_____

_____

_____

_____

_____

_____

Is your treatment of others based on their actions and behaviors toward you? Or are they based on your moods/feelings? Is your treatment based on the present relationship status or past feelings or issues with them?

_____

_____

Growth takes courage, patience, time, focused intention, and repetition.

_____

_____

_____

_____

_____

_____

_____

_____

_____

_____

It's never too late to be who you are meant to be and to do what you've always dreamed of doing. All it takes is a decision. Every day that you wake up is a new beginning and an opportunity to take small steps in the direction of your dream life.

Would you consider your relationships to be healthy or unhealthy as a whole? Do your relationships add happiness to your life, or do you view them as a source of stress? Why?

_____

_____

_____

Handle others with love and compassion, we are all recovering from something.

_____

_____

_____

_____

_____

_____

_____

_____

Spend more time indulging in the simple pleasures of life.
Make room for the people, things, and thoughts that
bring and keep a smile on your face.

Exercise: OBSERVING YOUR TREATMENT OF YOU

How do you normally treat yourself? Do you have a self-care routine? What is it? How often do you practice it? If not, how do you preserve you?

_____

_____

_____

_____

_____

_____

_____

_____

_____

_____

Incorporate your needs as well as the needs of others for a healthy life balance. You matter and need the warmth of your own love sometimes.

You attract who you are, not what you want.

How do you celebrate your wins? How do you treat yourself when you fall short of your goals or expectations? Are they positive or negative?

_____

_____

_____

_____

Become the person you'd want to be with. It all starts with you.

_____

_____

_____

_____

_____

_____

_____

_____

Compare how you treat others with how you treat yourself? Is it the same? Do you treat others better than you treat yourself? If you have more positives than negatives, write down some ideas of how to improve.

Don't try to change anyone else. Instead look for ways to keep improving and ways you can change your interaction with others for the better.

Check-in Time: PERSONAL REFLECTION

Use the next few pages to take time to reflect on the things that we've covered in this section and what you've discovered about yourself and your experiences so far. How are you feeling? What can you do to reward yourself for your courage and commitment to your healing? Do it!

_____

_____

_____

_____

_____

_____

_____

_____

_____

Learning how to properly love and care for yourself teaches others how to properly love you. Teach by example.

AFFIRMATION: I am attracting good things & people to me.

_____

_____

_____

_____

_____

_____

_____

_____

_____

_____

_____

_____

_____

Take responsibility for yourself, your feelings,
your vibe, and your treatment of others.

AFFIRMATION: I am growing into the best version of myself.

Kindness, love, compassion, patience, and gentleness are invaluable gifts you can give to others and yourself.

You're Not Alone

When it comes to being hurt, it can feel like such an isolated and lonely place to be. It's very easy to become so consumed by your pain and disappointment that you can't see or even process the outside world. You get so stuck on how you feel to the point that you feel like no one else could possibly understand your pain. It makes you feel like you don't have anyone to lean on.

However, I'm here to remind you, you're not alone. Let me say that again. You are not alone.

Other people are hurting too. Knowing this doesn't necessarily make your pain go away, but it can help you put things in perspective. I want you to really start to realize that your process of dealing with pain and hurt doesn't need to be a lonely one.

Listen, I love you. I want to see you win. I don't have to know you. I don't ever have to lay my eyes on you, however we're still somehow connected, and I want the best for you. I want you to be happy. I want you to be healed. I mean that from the bottom of my heart.

I want you to know that you have someone rooting for you.

In addition to my love and support, you also need to know that God loves you and God wants you in a better place.

It's very common to feel like even God has abandoned you in your moments of hurt and pain. You might question God's presence. Thinking, "Why has God allowed this to happen to me?"

Often, we turn our anger and resentment from our heartbreaks and other hurtful experiences toward God as well.

However, God is always present and always with you, no matter what you're going through or how you feel. The Bible says, "Give all your worries and cares to God, for He cares about you." 1 Peter 5:7, NLT

As you continue working through your healing and completing the exercises in this book, I want you to know you are supported.

When we're hurting, a lot of times we fail to realize or acknowledge the people who are in our lives, who deeply care for us. We don't allow ourselves to fully experience their love and support or fully grasp it, not because their love and support for us doesn't exist, but because we aren't allowing them to see our struggle.

We're not being transparent and honest with them about the fact that we need help and a shoulder to cry on.

You might be putting on a persona that you've got it all together. That you're fine. That everything in your life is amazing. When that's not really what's going on. That's not how you're really feeling at all.

For you to be able to receive the help you need and the support you so desperately desire, you must be open and honest about your struggle. You can't hide behind your "I'm so strong, I've got it all together" mask.

You're still strong, even more so when you're going through.

You're not required to have it all together all the time.

Ish happens. Period. It's nothing to be ashamed of.

It's important to let people in. You need to be supported during times when you're hurting.

When you open yourself up and allow the right people to see your struggles, your test will become your testimony.

This healing process might feel like hell and seem as if everything is falling apart, however, it's really the look of true change and growth. You need to get past the ugly layers in order for your truly beautiful parts to shine through. Once it's all said and done, you'll one day be able to appreciate looking back at the process and your strength to endure.

When this happens and you're able to share your story without shame or guilt, it can have a huge impact on other people's lives. That's the beautiful thing about healing and being transparent about what you've gone through. You're then equipped to help other people.

Our healing is powerful enough to help other people break their cycles of pain, hurt, and disappointment. We're all better together.

Exercise: TUNING INTO YOUR FEELINGS

Do you often feel alone or lonely? When you have these feelings do you reach out to people you trust for help? Who?

_____

_____

_____

_____

_____

How do you frequently deal with feelings of sadness or loneliness?

_____

_____

_____

_____

_____

_____

Are you allowing the people you trust and are close to you to see the real going on in your life? If not, why do you feel you need to put on a façade?

_____

_____

Your time is coming.

_____

_____

_____

_____

_____

_____

_____

_____

_____

The best romantic relationships have a foundation of friendship.

Review your list of how you deal with your feelings of loneliness. Do these habits help or hinder your emotional state?

_____

_____

_____

_____

_____

_____

What are some more positive alternatives you can use to work through these emotions? List a few people you trust that could assist you.

_____

_____

_____

_____

_____

_____

Fall in love with healing yourself.

Do you find it easy or difficult to reach out to others when you're experiencing difficult times in your life? Do you naturally go inward? Why?

_____

_____

_____

_____

_____

_____

Do you pray to help you ground yourself in God during your difficult life experiences? Why or Why not?

_____

_____

_____

_____

_____

"Give all your cares to God, for he cares for you".
–1 PETER 5:7, NLT

Check-in Time: PERSONAL REFLECTION

Use the next several pages to take time to reflect on the things that we've covered in this section and what you've discovered about yourself and your experiences. How are you feeling? What can you do to reward yourself for your courage and commitment to your healing? Do it!

_____

_____

_____

_____

_____

_____

_____

_____

_____

When you have God, you have everything.
When you have everything, you shouldn't worry about anything.

AFFIRMATION: I accept myself just as I am.

_____

_____

_____

_____

_____

_____

_____

_____

_____

Faith and fear can't coexist. Every day, you must make a choice between living from a place of fear or of faith. Choose wisely.

_____

_____

_____

_____

_____

AFFIRMATION: I accept the lessons my pain &
hurt are teaching me.

_____

_____

_____

_____

_____

_____

_____

_____

_____

_____

_____

Date yourself. Talk sweetly to yourself.
Get to know how it feels so you are prepared and
able to receive it from your future love. Practice on you.

PART II

THE Release

PROCESSING YOUR

Pain & Hurtful

EXPERIENCES

Healing Declaration:
"I Am Healing. I Am Healed."

Understanding the Physical Experience of Release

Any type of detox, cleansing, or healing work you do will result in some type of release. This can happen on a physical, mental, emotional, or spiritual level, and often happens on several levels at the same time.

I mentioned in *Love After...Vol. I* how my healing method was similar to a physical detox, but it targets the emotions instead. Just like with a detox that targets your body, an emotional detox will cause your body to release toxins that have been trapped within your pores, muscles, organs, etc.

Everything is connected. It's important for you to understand this concept. Everything we experience, we experience in layers. There is an emotional response to everything we experience physically and vice versa. There are going to be levels to your healing and layers of your release.

As you continue to work through the exercises in this book, you'll be releasing negative emotions and the equivalent of these emotions that have manifested and gotten trapped in various parts of your body.

When toxins and toxic energy are released, your body and mind have to deal with a sudden and powerful shift in balance. It's impossible to experience a release in any one of your bodies (physical, emotional, spiritual, mental) and not have the other bodies affected.

The physical experience you might go through as a result of your natural healing and emotional release is often referred to as a "Healing Crisis." The medical term for healing crisis is the "Herxheimer Reaction." This occurs when the cells release toxins into circulation but the elimination organs (skin, lungs, liver, kidneys, bladder & GI tract) are not able to eliminate them quickly enough.

Don't be alarmed. While you're releasing the old unhealthy, negative, and toxic energy that has been trapped within you, your body will need time to adjust because you're changing internally. Your physical, mental, and emotional self will need to figure out how to balance with each shift you make on your healing journey. While this is happening, you're likely going to experience uncomfortable symptoms in your body.

A *Healing Crisis* is going to vary depending on the person. It might even take you a while to identify and connect the two.

Initially you might not realize that what's happening in your body is a direct result of your self-healing work actually working. Removing the negative emotions of anger, hurt, a broken heart, unhealed trauma, unspoken feelings, betrayal, rejection, and loss need to also be removed from where they got lodged in your body as well. In other words, your body will respond to your efforts to get the gunk out of you completely.

Remember that it's all a part of the process and essential, really, to your true and complete healing.

Up until now, your body was maintaining and operating in basically an unhealthy and imbalanced state based on all these feelings being stuck in your physical and emotional body. If you've ever said to yourself, "I feel off," that's probably why.

Once you work to get everything realigned and balanced it's going to take your mind, body, and emotions time to adjust. It's nothing to fear or a reason to abort your mission of continuing your healing journey. The name is just a title given to the process your physical body goes through when releasing negativity and toxins from your system.

Again, you might experience a lot of different emotions during this time. However, the physical symptoms of a *Healing Crisis* usually take the form of liquids.

Physical Release Symptoms Might Include:

- Tears, or crying for no apparent reason. You might not be sad or upset but the tears may just need to fall. This is normal.

- Perspiration. You may not normally sweat a lot but during this process you might sweat more. This can also include night sweats. Again, toxins are getting released from your body.

- Excess saliva. You may wake up with dried saliva on your face/pillow as a result of your mouth being more moist than normal.

- Diarrhea. Again, the crap has to come out. You might experience it for a few days. Don't panic. Stay hydrated.

Other physical ways your body might respond to the new normal you're trying to create with your healing work is fatigue, muscle ache, nausea, inflammation, and vomiting.

Emotional Release Symptoms Might Include:

- Picking fights with loved ones (Resist this one and use a positive alternative you worked on above instead).

- Letting go of thoughts and feelings that held you back.

- Feeling the need to set a broken relationship straight.

- Feeling heavy.

- Depression and/or anxiety.

- A large emotional purge.

You've probably heard the saying before; "things often have to get worse before they can get better." The same applies here. You might be thinking, "Why in the world should I go through with this if it's going to make me feel worse than I feel now?"

Listen, the reality is your body is most likely operating from a sick place already. You don't realize it or it's not as obvious because it's become your normal state of being.

Healing requires you to temporarily experience "sick symptoms" in order for your body to rid itself of the actual cause of the sickness.

Symptoms express the body's attempt to heal but are not the cause of your body's unhealthy state. Remember, our goal here is not to keep focusing on and only treating your symptoms. We're aiming to get to the root issues and dig them up, so that healthier seeds can be planted in their place.

I don't want to scare you or deter you, but I'm always going to keep it real and be honest with you. I'm laying it out for you plainly so that you can be aware of what's going on below the surface and internally as you self-heal. These are things that "might" happen.

Everyone is different. Remember me telling you before that results and processes will vary because everyone is at a different place in the pain spectrum. I'm giving you all this information not for you to run in the opposite direction, but so that you are aware of what's going on and can be proactive and also patient with yourself and this entire process.

Depending on how deeply your pain is rooted within you, there is a chance that you might not experience any symptoms of a *Healing Crisis* when you first start your healing journey. However, later as you work through tougher issues, you might notice your body's release. It's normal to begin experiencing symptoms within 48-72 hours. However, it could be a longer range. It honestly just depends on you and your body.

It's important that you pay attention to yourself and how you're feeling. You may think it's something you ate or a movie or television show you watched that has you bothered or your stomach upset. However, if you've done healing work, there is a good chance it's your body releasing the negative toxins and energy and that you're getting the release you need.

Again, the more you are aware of the interconnectedness of yourself, the better you'll be able to handle the natural responses of your mind, body, and spirit.

If any of the above symptoms occur in the days and weeks following your self-healing work, be encouraged; it's a true sign of healing.

The deeper and more intense a *Healing Crisis* is, the deeper and more intense your healing will be, and the more likely you'll be free from what had you bound.

Exercise: TUNING INTO YOU- SENSORY

How are you feeling? What are you feeling? Be descriptive here.

_____

_____

_____

_____

_____

What are you hearing? Are you taking time to listen to yourself?

_____

_____

_____

_____

_____

_____

Stay focused and keep moving forward in faith.
The payoff is coming!

Exercise: RECOGNIZING YOUR PHYSICAL/ EMOTIONAL RELEASE

Have you noticed yourself experiencing any of the symptoms of release from the above list?

_____

_____

_____

_____

_____

If so, how long between doing healing work do the symptoms occur?

_____

_____

_____

_____

_____

Things to Remember:

- Drink plenty of water as well as drinks with electrolytes to stay really hydrated. Since your body releases toxins and negative emotions via fluids, it's important for you to replenish yourself with liquids. It's a good habit to develop if you don't already work proactively to hydrate. Drinking lots of water will also assist your body in flushing the toxins and negativity out. It's important to replace what you lose.

- Eat properly. Food is fuel and medicine. Make sure you eat well and keep your energy up. This will help combat fatigue and general signs of low-energy, heaviness, etc.

- Pay attention to how you're feeling during this process. I've included space at the end of each chapter for you to journal and check in with yourself about your feelings and your journey. Writing will help you go deeper within and will assist you as you work out your feelings. It's also a part of your release.

- Listen to yourself and your intuition. If you've read any of my other books, you know I'm big on this. You will get a lot of clarity and insight during this time. Don't doubt and second guess what comes to you.

Listen and follow directions. It's always for your own good, health, and protection.

Okay, now that you're more prepared for what's to come, we're going to take this healing journey to the next level.

Remember, trust and have faith. Stay committed and get the healing you need by doing the work.

In Philippian 3:13-14, Paul encourages us to be strong in our faith, declaring, "I have not yet achieved it, but I focus on this one thing: Forgetting the past and looking forward to what lies ahead, I press on to reach the end of the race and receive the heavenly prize for which God, through Christ Jesus, is calling us."

Keep going! Keep pressing! There is a light at the end of this tunnel and a prize of overall better health in all areas of your life waiting for you as you continue to go forward. Stay focused on what lies ahead.

Check-in Time: PERSONAL REFLECTION

Use the next few pages to take time to reflect on the things that we've covered in this section and what you've discovered about yourself and your experiences so far. How are you feeling? What can you do to reward yourself for your courage and commitment to your healing? Do it!

_____

_____

_____

_____

_____

Your body is where you live for life. Take care of your body and it will take care of you.

_____

_____

_____

_____

_____

_____

AFFIRMATION: I am willing to see things differently.

_____

_____

_____

_____

_____

_____

_____

_____

_____

_____

_____

_____

_____

Stay focused and keep moving forward in faith.
The payoff is coming!

AFFIRMATION: I give myself permission to heal.

_____

_____

_____

_____

_____

_____

_____

_____

_____

_____

_____

_____

_____

Your body loves you so much it works 24/7 to keep you alive.
Your participation is needed if you want to be alive and well.

Put the Hurt Out in Front of You

A good portion of our lives are spent running from our issues. We live our lives trying to ignore the things that bother us and work hard to convince ourselves and others that we're good. We lie to ourselves and others, by repeating, "I'm fine." When we're not fine or even close to it most of the time.

Trying to convince yourself that you don't have any problems, that "it" isn't affecting you anymore or that the unresolved issues are no longer issues in your life is a waste of time and energy. The same time and energy you could use to deal with and heal yourself from the actual issues negatively affecting you.

Of course, you can tell yourself whatever you want to hear. However, your behavior, your energy, your mindset, all these things will tell a different, deeper story. They will betray your words and show others that something *is* going on within you.

Let's start to identify the deeper things holding you back and start to pull them out. It's important that you put the hurt out in front of you. Stop making excuses or trying to convince yourself you aren't struggling in some areas. It's important to allow yourself this time to properly identify and work through your pain points so that you can establish the new normal of operating from a healthy place in life.

On pages 90-93 in *Love After Heartbreak, Vol. I* there is an example "Who Hurt Me List" for you to refer to as a reference for you to write your own.

Exercise: MY WHO HURT ME LIST(S)

Below take time to ask yourself the question, "Who Hurt Me?" Then listen for the answers. People and experiences will begin to come to mind. Write the name of each person and each experience down as a list. Be as specific as possible when writing out the details of the experience.

PERSON 1 | Experience 1:

_____

_____

_____

_____

PERSON 2 | Experience 2:

_____

_____

_____

_____

You are worth your effort. You are worth your attention. You are worth your love. You are worth your time. You are worth healing.

PERSON 3 | Experience 3:

_____

_____

_____

_____

_____

PERSON 4 | Experience 4:

_____

_____

_____

_____

_____

PERSON 5 | Experience 5:

_____

_____

_____

_____

_____

PERSON 6 | Experience 6:

_____

_____

_____

_____

_____

PERSON 7 | Experience 7:

_____

_____

_____

_____

_____

You might need more room to complete your lists. This is perfectly okay. Grab a few sheets of notebook paper and continue for as long as you need to. Once you've completed your list(s) fold them up and insert them in this chapter, so they are all in the same place for future use. You will need to reference them in the next step of my healing process.

Take a moment and just thank yourself for your courage to work through and write out your lists. It can be scary to confront your pain and to address your past issues and resist the urge to run away from them.

This is one of the reasons why I want you to fully complete this exercise. The reality is that because we fear facing ourselves, our hurt, and our past, we run. We've been running from things for so long it's become a part of our natural behavior.

However, you're reading this book because it's finally time to stop running and face things once and for all. No more suppressing your feelings. You heal by releasing, not suppressing. Taking the time to write out your "who hurt me list" is a necessary process of releasing.

Do not hold back with this list. Truly allow yourself to go there. You need this release and complete healing like you need air to breathe. Allow yourself to open up. Chances are you've got a lot bottled up that needs to be released.

Also, don't be surprised by what comes out when you really go deep within and ask yourself the question, "who hurt me?" This exercise might trigger a strong emotional response. Relax. Breathe through it. It's normal. It's healthy. It's a part of your release.

Granted, that's not what we want, it's what we've been avoiding, but know that it's for your overall good.

Be patient with yourself. Be kind, gentle, and loving with yourself.

Give yourself permission to grieve the experience(s), especially if you haven't ever really dealt with them. This can be difficult because it can often feel like we're having to live the experience all over again.

However, by not dealing with each experience properly, you've subconsciously held the memory and have been reliving it one way or another when triggered. At least this time, it is to rid yourself of the emotions attached to each experience so you can properly heal, and the open wound can finally close.

Check-in Time: PERSONAL REFLECTION

Use the next few pages to take time to reflect on the things that we've covered in this section and what you've discovered about yourself and your experiences so far. How are you feeling? What can you do to reward yourself for your courage and commitment to your healing? Do it!

_____

_____

_____

_____

_____

_____

Be gentle with you.
Handle yourself with
care and compassion
throughout this
process.

_____

_____

_____

_____

AFFIRMATION: I am my own source of
happiness, joy, and fulfillment.

_____

_____

_____

_____

_____

_____

_____

_____

_____

_____

_____

_____

_____

Release the need to put expectations on yourself during your journey.
Allow things to just be what they are going to and need to be for you.

AFFIRMATION: I have the power to create
the life I want to live now.

_Surrender the
need to control
the process or
outcome._

Get Things Off Your Chest

When you suppress your negative emotions and aren't open and honest about your true feelings, you're basically in bondage to lies and deceit. All these things are paralyzing you. They're keeping you from moving forward and living your best life.

In order to free yourself, you must speak your truth. You need to release the truth into the atmosphere. Let it come out of you. This is how you're going to continue on the path to healing.

Speaking your truth allows you to acknowledge your real issues. When you acknowledge your real issues, you can face them. Once you're able to face them, you'll be able to conquer them, learn from them, and become better from them.

You cannot fix something that you won't acknowledge exists. You can't overcome an obstacle if you keep telling yourself there are no obstacles.

Be as honest as possible with yourself during this process.

In *Love After Heartbreak, Vol. I*, I discussed the benefits of seeking out a helping professional to work with for talking through your past hurtful experiences, in order to release them into the atmosphere and get them off your chest.

This chapter coincides with the letter writing release that is a part of my healing method. Since you may or may not send the letters to the people you're writing them to, you don't need to spend time writing them out here in your journal.

However, I want you to spend some time learning how to center yourself and listen to yourself so you can get reacquainted with you.

We spend most of our time centered in the external. We're so distracted in our every day lives that it's hard to really spend time listening to ourselves and figuring out our needs, wants, likes and dislikes.

Just like with anything else, these things change over time.

What you wanted and needed in your teen years are much different when you get into your 20s, 30s, and so on. If you're still depending on your past you to figure out what you want and need now, it's likely you're frustrated and unhappy with your current results on all levels.

You need to get to know the you, you are today.

Taking the time to listen to yourself, paying attention to the small things, and observing your feelings, are all ways you can use to get to know yourself better. Again, self-discovery is a key component to thriving, loving relationships.

How can someone else make you happy, if you don't know how to make you happy? The other person is depending on you to tell them what happiness means to you, so they can do it. If you have no clue what that looks like for you, the person's time and efforts will be in vain. You'll both end up frustrated. Time and energy is wasted, and the hurt people, hurt people cycle continues. It's unnecessary and avoidable.

However, since you're now committed to tuning into you and allowing yourself space and time to answer the same questions that others might ask you in order to get to know you better, you'll be prepared to accurately share with someone else what your needs are.

We've been focused on the deep things because too much time has already been given to the surface stuff.

It's still important for you to complete the letter writing exercises I laid out for you in *Love After Heartbreak, Vol. I.* However, in addition to them, I also want you to spend some time answering the following questions. These questions will help you really get a good picture of the you, you've been, so that you can see how you've played a part in every outcome of your life and relationships. Sure, others participated, but this is not about them. It's about you, which is the only thing you can control and change.

Exercise: LISTENING & TUNING INTO YOU

Do you feel pressured to please people? Why?

_____

_____

_____

_____

_____

_____

_____

*Love waters
the soul.*

_____

_____

_____

_____

_____

How do you see yourself in relationships? Do you go into it looking for someone else to make you happy and to fulfill you?

_____

_____

_____

_____

_____

Do you feel like you have things to offer? What are they? Are you a giver or a taker in relationships?

_____

_____

_____

_____

_____

_____

Do you take up for yourself & demand respect from others? Why/Not?

_____

_____

_____

_____

_____

_____

Do you often feel like the victim in situations? Why?

_____

_____

_____

_____

_____

_____

_____

What does being happy and fulfilled look like to you? Do you feel you need someone else in order to achieve a happy and fulfilled life?

_____

_____

_____

_____

_____

How can you make yourself happy and fulfilled?

_____

_____

_____

_____

_____

_____

You have to be and give love in order to attract love to you.

Tuning into yourself is important on a daily basis. However, tuning out is just as important. The more you get clear and aligned with who you are now and who you are becoming, you need to be equally aware of the things you're consuming that aren't serving your new path.

Many of this comes in the form of what and who we listen to. I'm not just talking about music here. I'm talking about other people's opinions. Ridicule, projected fears, other people's toxic energy, as well as our own inner voice that has been repeating self-defeating messages to us for our entire lives.

It's not just other people's damage that you need to be released from. You have to release yourself from your own inner negative voice that has stifled and discouraged you and that keeps you blocked from liking and loving yourself completely.

A lot of times we are our own worst enemies. Our internal dialogue is mean, judgmental, and limiting. We probably would never let someone else talk to us the same way we are in the habit of talking to ourselves. It's time to take a look at the things that you need to tune out in order to be the best version of your new self.

Exercise: TUNING OUT THE NEGATIVE YOU

What are some of the things you say to yourself on a regular basis? Be completely honest here. Are you in the habit of talking sweet to yourself or are your words often bitter and judgmental?

Your ability to love is a gift. It should be given away freely and without strings attached.

_____

_____

_____

_____

_____

_____

_____

_____

_____

_____

In what areas of your life has your own negative self-talk hindered you? Has it affected you in your relationships? Career? Dreams? Physical health? Experiences?

_____

_____

_____

_____

_____

_____

_____

_____

_____

Your healing on a level deeper than what your mind can comprehend. You're accessing a deeper "knowing" within and locating your internal peace.

_____

_____

Is the negative self-talk in your head, your voice or someone else's voice? Is it easier to believe positive or negative things about yourself?

What do you need to hear instead?

One of the most amazing feelings in the world is getting to the point of accepting yourself, speaking lovingly to yourself, and looking in the mirror and actually liking the person staring back at you.

Recognizing Self-Sabotage
in Your Self-Talk

These exercises aren't meant to make you feel bad. They are meant to help you become aware of what's going on within you. The reality is when you take time to really look within, it's not all roses and sunshine. Looking within requires you to have the courage to face some of the dark places that dwell in all of us.

Looking at how you talk to yourself or how you've chosen to view yourself allows you to find the courage to make the changes needed to overcome this type of self-sabotage. It's not always others that are out to hurt us. Sometimes we work hard to hurt ourselves.

Self-sabotaging behaviors are often hidden in our everyday thoughts. Simply put, self-sabotage is when part of your personality acts in conflict with another part of your personality.

Psychology Today defines self-sabotage as behavior that creates problems in our life and interferes with long-standing goals. The most common self-sabotaging behaviors include procrastination, self-medication with drugs or alcohol, and comfort eating. These behaviors are all direct forms of self-injury and are extremely harmful. These acts may offer temporary relief in the moment, but they ultimately work against us and add to whatever problem we're using them to treat.

Usually when we're engaging in self-sabotaging behaviors, we're also choosing to have a victim mentality. A victim mentality includes blaming others and pointing the finger at someone else as the cause of why we're acting out this way. Doing this keeps us stuck. It doesn't encourage us to make the needed changes within ourselves. A victim mentality helps to keep us defeated, unhappy, and unhealthy.

5 Ways to Silence Your Inner Critic

It's important to learn how to silence your inner critic and tune it out. Begin practicing better self-talk habits by practicing the following.

- Learn to observe every negative thought.

- Find out where it's coming from (usually a place of fear).

- Stop it. Say, "nope." Say it in your head or out loud.

- Flip it. Change the negative statement around into a positive one.

- Add more positive language into your vocabulary. Instead of saying words like, have to, made to, or forced. Choose to say, encouraged, choosing, decided. Be intentional with your words.

The more you practice these small changes in behavior, the better you'll get at them. You are not meant to be run by your emotions. However, if you don't control how you think about yourself, how you think about yourself will continue to run and ruin your life.

Check-in Time: PERSONAL REFLECTION

Use the next few pages to take time to reflect on the things that we've covered in this section and what you've discovered about yourself and your experiences so far. How are you feeling? What can you do to reward yourself for your courage and commitment to your healing? Do it!

_____

_____

_____

_____

_____

_____

_____

Transformation is a slow and steady process that can't be rushed. Be kind to yourself. Your healed self is worth waiting for and working toward.

_____

_____

_____

AFFIRMATION: I am beautiful both inside and out.

_____

_____

_____

_____

_____

_____

_____

_____

_____

_____

_____

_____

_____

Your smile is your greatest and most alluring accessory. Where it often..

AFFIRMATION: I am allowed to say no, it's a part of my self-care?

Relax and trust that things are working out for you. Everything you want also wants you. Believe it to receive it.

"You are God's masterpiece."
–Ephesians 2:10, NLT

PART III

DAILY PRACTICE

Experiencing

DEEPER

Healing

Healing Declaration:
"I Am Healing. I Am Healed."

Practicing Forgiveness is Key

Forgiveness is a form of release. When you forgive someone, you're saying, "I'm no longer going to hold on to the negative feelings and energy of a situation or the anger I have towards a person any longer."

Forgiving someone doesn't' mean you're saying what they did is okay, acceptable, or that you're going to let it slide. Understand that forgiveness doesn't mean you're co-signing the experience or person.

Forgiveness is a choice. Your choice. It's your decision to forgive someone, which empowers you to take back control over your life, your emotions, and your healing.

The act of forgiveness simply means, "I'm not going to keep holding on to this."

Unforgiveness is like holding poison in your hands and waiting for the other person to drink it. Whether you realize it or not, you're the person most affected and further damaged by unforgiveness. The person who hurt you probably isn't suffering because you didn't forgive them. So, if you think not forgiving someone is revenge or payback for their wrong toward you, it's not. Plain and simple.

In *Love After Heartbreak, Vol. I*, I go in depth about two types of forgiveness, forgiving others and forgiving yourself.

However, saying you've forgiven someone isn't enough to remove the emotional hurt attached to the situation or the person. Practicing forgiveness is also not an instant pain reliever. Again, it's going to take practice to distance yourself and your emotions from the hurt attached to the experiences and people who have hurt you in the past. It's also going to take conscious choice. You will need to make the decision to actively forgive in your heart and your mind each time you feel negative emotions around your past experiences.

"Forgiveness is a releasing of emotional guilt you place upon the other person. It's a choice. It happens in the heart. It's not a release of responsibility or an absence of healthy boundaries. It doesn't even mean justice or reconciliation. It is, however, a conscious choice to remove the right to get even from the person who injured you. It's a release of anger and any bitterness or grudge." Ron Edmondson

Some experiences and people are going to be easier to forgive than others. However, I want you to remember that everything is forgivable. Mainly because it's your choice. You have control over whether or not you choose to forgive someone and the hurtful experience.

Also, it's important to note that when you're holding unforgiveness toward someone you're automatically associating yourself with negative emotions. Below is a list of the ten most common negative emotions, followed by a list of the ten most common positive emotions. Unforgiveness waters the seeds of negativity that causes emotional stress within you. If you've taken time to work through the rest of the steps in my healing process, do you really want to cancel out all your hard work due to unforgiveness?

Remember, unforgiveness is a death sentence. You are literally choosing to kill yourself because as I mentioned earlier everything you experience emotionally plays out physically. Toxic energy turns into disease and illness when you leave it unchecked.

The 10 most common negative emotions are:

- Anger
- Sadness
- Jealousy
- Hatred
- Grief

- Isolation
- Humiliation
- Worthlessness
- Anxiety
- Conflict

The 10 most common positive emotions are:

- Joy
- Gratitude
- Serenity
- Interest
- Hope

- Pride
- Amusement
- Inspiration
- Awe
- Love

Believe it or not, you are in control of your emotions. Sure, you won't always feel 100% positive every minute of every day. However, a healthy balance to try to keep is a 3:1 ratio. So, for every negative emotion you experience, you should try to counterbalance it with three positive emotions.

Studies show that even one five-minute episode of anger is so stressful that it can damage your immune system for more than six hours! Imagine a lifetime worth!

Forgiveness and letting go of the negative emotions associated with the hurt will allow you to counterbalance things and get on track to better overall health.

Forgiveness is tricky because we tend to forgive people in our minds. However, forgiveness has to do with your heart. If you've been hurt repeatedly, it's only natural for you to put up a wall around your heart so that you won't continue to be hurt. However, your wall is a barrier that's hindering you from the good things in life. Forgiveness helps to chip away at the wall, so it doesn't keep love away.

Exercise: MEASURING YOUR FORGIVENESS

Go back through your full "Who Hurt Me List" and re-read the experiences and people you have listed. Pay attention to how you feel when reviewing what you wrote. On a scale of one (unforgiveness) to ten (complete forgiveness) think about what your rating was for each experience/person before you began your healing journey with this book and *Love After Heartbreak, Vol. I.*

On the side of each person/experience write down the number that measures your level of forgiveness toward what happened before you began your healing journey and now that you're in the process of self-healing.

Be completely honest. Again, this is a non-judgment zone.

Hopefully, your number is a little higher now than when you first started on your healing journey. Make a point to revisit your list periodically in the future and re-read your "Who Hurt Me List" to see if your numbers increase over time. Every time you revisit your list, write down the updated number in a different color or put the date with it so that you'll be able to readily see your progress over time.

My prayer is that your numbers will continue to rise, the healthier you become.

Exercise #2: MEASURING YOUR FORGIVENESS

Forgiveness is a decision. It's not an automatic healer of your emotions. However, without forgiveness, you won't be able to truly heal over time. Below are four ways to tell if you've really forgiven someone. Go back through your "Who Hurt Me" list and ask yourself the following questions. You'll know immediately whether or not you're free from unforgiveness based on your body's reaction (facial expressions, shrugs, eye roll) and your natural responses to the questions. Pay attention to yourself here.

Is your first thought about them positive or negative?

When the first thought you have about them is not the injury they caused in your life, you have probably extended forgiveness. However, if you think about them in terms of your hurt and pain, it's probably because you have some more healing and forgiveness to work through.

Would you help them?

If you knew they were in trouble and you had the ability, would you help them? If your first thought is, "Hell no. I hope they die." It's safe to say, there's more work needed. Even though you're not obligated to help anyone, if you would extend a hand to a person that's hurt you, it's a sign you've forgiven them. Even if you'd pass on helping them but know in your heart that you also don't wish any negativity toward them, this is a good sign of forgiveness as well.

Do you want revenge?

Do you think of getting even with the person? There are circumstances where people do things that might merit retaliation. However, if you feel you need to help the person pay the consequences for their actions, it's probably because you're holding on to unforgiveness. Hurting someone else also hurts yourself. Remember that. Give them to God. He'll handle it and you won't have to suffer any consequences by taking matters into your own hands.

Do you want to see them fail?

Again, the hurt people, hurt people cycle is real. However, wishing injury or failure on someone who harms or hurts us is only adding to the cycle. God instructs us to pray for our enemies. Prayer is a form of release.

I realize these questions might be tough. There are probably people and experiences on your "Who Hurt Me List" that are causing you difficulty in practicing the forgiveness process.

However, it's important that you focus on them in your prayers. Ask God to continue to work on your heart and to give you peace in these areas.

You can begin actively practicing forgiveness today. The more you practice, the better you will get at it. The more you pray about it and ask God to change your heart, the more you will release the burden that you're carrying from it.

God will be able to give you peace in place of the emotional pain that unforgiveness is using to torment you. The more peace you have about it, the less of an emotional charge it will have on you. You'll diminish its hold on you. This is how you get your power back and live fully and completely in the present.

You'll be able to recognize and enjoy the wonderful things that are happening to and for you right now.

Exercise: PRACTICING FORGIVENESS

Below is a prayer I want you to pray for every single person that you wrote down on your WHM list. Verbally fill in the blanks, by saying the names of the people and what happened, instead of writing them out again. The blank lines are there to hold space for you and the experience.

I believe it will be more beneficial to you to say the prayer out loud vs. silently. You need to hear yourself say it. The words need to penetrate through you and help you release any additional emotional residue that may still be tied to the person and experience.

You don't have to go through your entire list in one sitting. Take your time and go at a pace that is comfortable for you. However, make sure you get through the entire list eventually. I also recommend highlighting the names and experiences that you feel you've healed from and offered forgiveness to. Keep going through your list until you have your entire list highlighted. That's the goal. To extend forgiveness and practice it with everyone on your list.

Forgiveness Prayer

_____, I forgive you for all of the ways that you have hurt me whether it was physically, emotionally, mentally, spiritually, sexually, financially or in any other way, knowingly or unknowingly, in the past, present or future through thought, word or deed; by _____(e.g. describe their negative words or actions or how their words or actions affected you). God, help me to develop a forgiving heart and spirit. Thank you. *Amen.*

Exercise: PRACTICING SELF-FORGIVENESS

Did you include yourself on your "Who Hurt Me List"? A lot of the unforgiveness that you hold against others, you're probably also holding against yourself as well. Take a moment and reflect on the things you need to forgive you for and write them in the spaces below. If you need more room use the reflection space at the end of this chapter or grab notebook paper to continue.

I forgive myself for _____

I forgive myself for _____

I forgive myself for _____

I forgive myself for _____

I forgive myself for _____

I forgive myself for _____

I forgive myself for _____

I forgive myself for _____

I forgive myself for _____

Self-Forgiveness Prayer

Pray this short prayer for your self-forgiveness while looking in the mirror and hugging yourself.

Please forgive me for all of the ways in which I have hurt you, physically, emotionally, mentally, psychically, spiritually, sexually, financially or in any other way, knowingly or unknowingly through thought, word or deed. God, help me to continually forgive myself and others. Help me to let go of the memories associated with my pain so that I can experience all the wonderful things you have in store for my life now and going forward. God, thank you for loving me even when I was unloving to myself. Thank you for being patient with me. *Amen.*

Check-in Time: PERSONAL REFLECTION

Use the next few pages to take time to reflect on the things that we've covered in this section and what you've discovered about yourself and your experiences so far. How are you feeling? What can you do to reward yourself for your courage and commitment to your healing? Do it!

_____

_____

_____

_____

_____

_____

Every day you get a clean slate to begin anew. God doesn't hold anything over your head and neither should you.

_____

_____

_____

_____

_____

AFFIRMATION: I am deserving of love.

_____

_____

_____

_____

_____

_____

_____

_____

_____

_____

_____

_____

_____

"Come to me, all you who are weary and burdened, and I will give you rest. Take my yoke upon you...and you will find rest for your souls. For my yoke is easy and my burden is light."
–Matthew 11:28-30, NIV

AFFIRMATION: I take full responsibility for my own happiness.

God loves you and wants to see you whole, healed, and prospering in your original state.

Change Your Mindset

Free will is a gift. You get to choose how you view things, how you think, how you act, and what you choose to hold on to. A large part of the battle of getting the love you deserve starts in your mind. When you understand that you always have a choice, you will be able to conquer negativity and move on from your hurt.

When it comes to healing from your past and overcoming past hurts and disappointments, 9 times out of 10 you will use your past to assess your present situation. Doing this paralyzes you and hinders you when it comes to the decisions you make in life including your relationships, career, health, etc., especially if it's mostly negative.

How you choose to look at the people, places, and things around you after you've been hurt effects your experiences when interacting with these things going forward, and ultimately shapes your future reality.

Our experiences begin to pull us in one direction or another, sometimes good, sometimes bad. It's easy to begin to attach a negative perception to your present and future experiences based off your past. In order to move out of the negative place that you've dwelled in, a place that hasn't gotten you the results you want, a place that hasn't brought you any happiness or peace, you're going to have to be willing to change your mindset.

Exercise: IDENTIFYING YOUR
NEGATIVE PERCEPTIONS

Use the space below to list your negative perceptions about people, places, and things (food, products, giving or helping others) based on an experience you've had or from you internalizing another person's experience (family, friends, programming).

_____

_____

_____

_____

_____

_____

_____

_____

_____

_____

_____

Exercise: LET GO & ALLOW

What negative perceptions are you now ready to let go of? Sure, it might take you some time and practice to fully change your perceptions. However, you can actively decide to begin changing feelings, thought patterns, and habits that aren't serving you. Use the space below to write out the things that you are now willing to let go of. Think about what you want to take the place of the things you're letting go. Example: I let go of my tendency to label people and allow myself to be open to learn others.

I let go of _____, I allow _____.

I let go of _____, I allow _____.

I let go of _____, I allow _____.

I let go of _____, I allow _____.

I let go of _____, I allow _____.

I let go of _____, I allow _____.

I let go of _____, I allow _____.

Check-in Time: PERSONAL REFLECTION

Use the next few pages to take time to reflect on the things that
we've covered in this section and what you've discovered about
yourself and your experiences so far. How are you feeling? What
can you do to reward yourself for your courage and commitment
to your healing? Do it!

_____

_____

_____

_____

_____

_____

_____

_____

_____

*"Forget the former
things, do not dwell
on the past..."*

–Isaiah 43:18

_____

_____

_____

AFFIRMATION: I speak to myself and others
with love and kindness.

_____

_____

_____

_____

_____

_____

_____

_____

_____

_____

_____

_____

*Don't miss out on the wonderful things God wants to do in
and through your life now because you're stuck worrying
about yesterday. It's over. You made it.*

AFFIRMATION: I respect myself and others.

_____

_____

_____

_____

_____

You are a miracle.
Your story matters.
You matter.
Everything about
you is unique
and valuable.

_____

_____

_____

_____

_____

_____

_____

_____

_____

Trust God, Not People

―――――✕―――――

"Do not put your trust in princes, in human beings,
who cannot save. Blessed are those whose help is the
God of Jacob; whose hope is in the Lord their God."
–Psalm 146:3-5, NIV

Putting 100% of your trust in any human being is just not realistic. It's not fair to them. It's not fair to you. God is the only being worthy of your complete trust. God is not a man that He will lie. God will not let you down. God loves you unconditionally and He wants you to live an abundant life with everything good He has in store for you.

By shifting your focus to trusting your Spirit, you then begin to trust God and not people.

When you start to put more trust in God and your Spirit rather than in people, you'll be able to make better decisions. You'll be able to live a healthier, happier life. You'll also be able to avoid a lot of the hurt and damage that creates the need to have to heal in the first place.

So, what does trusting God and your Spirit really mean?

It Means You Don't Depend on You

The Bible tells us in Proverbs 3:5 to: "Trust in the LORD with all your heart and lean not on your own understanding."

The bottom line here is that you don't know better than God. You don't know how to manage your life, finances, job, family, and life responsibilities as well as you think you do.

You need God's help in every area of your life. This is how it's supposed to be because God wants to be in relationship with you. However, just like in human relationships, time, effort, and communication are all imperative in order to build your relationship with God. Relationship with God gives you the ability to trust Him with the life that He's given you to live.

It's safe to say that you probably wouldn't trust your life to people who you don't know. This may be the case with God as well. The only remedy to the lack of trust is relationship. You build relationship by spending time, communicating, and creating a bond. Get to know God for yourself. He will not disappoint and wants you to trust Him.

It Means Daily Prayer

God has called us to rest in His understanding, not to have all the answers. Each day we must consciously lay aside our own plans and expectations—and surrender to His plans and will for our lives.

The only way to know what God's plans are for our lives is to talk to Him on a consistent basis and ask. Going to God in prayer shows that you are wanting His input and will for your life. Pray before making decisions, plans, and everything in-between. The more you pray and spend time with God, the easier it will be for you to tune into the still, small voice God speaks to you in.

It Means Resisting the Desire to Reverse Course

Becoming dependent on God is very different from what we're used to. To be honest it takes time to adjust. However, I cannot tell you how much better your life will become just by putting this into practice. You can only develop new habits by doing the same things consistently over time.

Really trusting God in your everyday life requires a lifestyle shift. You're going to need to sideline your plans. Instead of asking God to co-sign your plans, you're going to discard your plans and ask God what He wants you to do instead.

Listening and obeying is just as important as prayer and asking God for direction. This will also require you to turn down the noise of other people's opinions. You're not going to be able to go to others for confirmation on what God tells you because they won't know what you're talking about. This is a good thing. It'll further help you lean in and trust God completely. Your desire should be to please God and God only.

It Means Reading God's Word & Obeying It

We rationalize a lot of things when our intuition tells us to do something we don't want to do. However, learning to trust God, means you're going to need to learn how to trust and obey your Spirit, which is God on the inside of you. You will need to put logic and reason on the backburner. God's direction won't always make sense.

Allow yourself to trust and have faith that all things are working out for your good. It doesn't need to make sense. You and God always have your best interest in mind. You and God are protective and loving toward you. It's only when you divert from your "first mind" or "intuitive voice" that you run into trouble. "Something" is the name we give God when we reflect and realize we made the wrong choice by not listening. "Something told me this was a bad idea. I should've listened."

God loves you. The more time you spend in His presence and reading His word, the more the voids you feel will be replaced by a foundational love that you can then reciprocate to yourself and others.

"Now faith is being sure of what you hope for and certain of what you do not see...Because anyone who comes to Him, must believe that He exists and rewards those who earnestly seek Him."
–Hebrews 11:1,6 NIV

Exercise: IDENTIFYING BARRIERS BLOCKING GOD

How often do you pray and seek God's guidance regarding your needs, plans, and decisions before making them? After making them?

_____

_____

_____

_____

_____

_____

Do you often use lack of time as an excuse of why you don't prioritize quiet time to spend with God? What are some other reasons you give yourself for not getting in relationship with God?

_____

_____

_____

_____

_____

Exercise: TRUSTING GOD MORE

In what areas of your life could you use God's help the most?

_____

_____

_____

_____

God wants you to want to spend time in His presence from a place of love and not obligation. How can you include prayer time in your schedule?

_____

_____

_____

_____

Write your own trusting God affirmation here. Say it daily.

_____

_____

_____

_____

Check-in Time: PERSONAL REFLECTION

Use the next few pages to take time to reflect on the things that we've covered in this section and what you've discovered about yourself and your experiences so far. How are you feeling? What can you do to reward yourself for your courage and commitment to your healing? Do it!

_____

_____

_____

If God is pleased with you, you shouldn't worry about who isn't.

_____

_____

_____

_____

_____

_____

AFFIRMATION: I like the me I am, and the me I am becoming.

_____

_____

_____

_____

_____

_____

_____

_____

_____

_____

_____

_____

_____

_Don't let your opinion or the opinions of others matter more to
you than God's opinion of you. God knows best, he made you._

AFFIRMATION: I own my feelings and won't allow
my emotions to run me.

_____

_____

_____

_____

_____   *God doesn't make*
mistakes. He does
_____   *everything for a*
reason and He
created you for
His glory.

_____

_____

_____

_____

_____

_____

_____

_____

Conclusion

Thank you for your courage and your persistence. Thank you for taking the journey within to get to a place of deeper self-discovery, which is the true ingredient needed for lasting transformation and healing.

Remember that healing is the first and most important step to take in finding love after heartbreak. We often want the results without the work. However, it doesn't work that way in life or in love. You get back what you put in. I want you to have it all and to be able to sustain the relationship of your dreams once you're blessed with it.

This is possibly the biggest missing piece of the puzzle. When it comes to getting that great, healthy, amazing relationship, it takes two great, healthy, amazing, whole individuals coming together as one.

Your healing is going to help you have a better relationship with yourself because that's the other foundational piece.

You've got to love yourself. Self-love is necessary. It's not selfish. If you're not good to you, you're not going to be good to anyone else. You're going to be wearing yourself out trying to give yourself to the wrong people, giving yourself for the wrong reasons, and you're going to produce the wrong results. It's important to break that cycle. I don't want you to be someone who continues to ignore your issues or suppress your negative emotions or unresolved pain. It's time to get better results.

Make room.

You're worth it. You deserve it. Completing all the exercises and taking time to reflect will ensure that you're completely ready to receive the information I will share in *Volume 2* of *Love After Heartbreak*.

Pray this prayer with me:

God, I pray you'll draw us closer to you. Teach us how to trust you beyond our senses and beyond our previous experiences. Move us forward in your promises for our lives. I pray God that this is a time of abundant harvest for your people who have planted, sowed, and labored in faith and tears.

God, I thank you now, by faith, for opening up the floodgates of heaven and pouring out your blessings on us where we won't have enough room to contain them all.

God, thank you for replenishing us with any virtues that were depleted as we were going through our storms. I pray you would strengthen our bond and connection with you now.

God, we love you. We trust you. We will begin to speak those things to come as though they are already. Your word says that you cause all things to work together for the good of those who love you.

We declare by faith now: We are healing, and we are healed. We are whole. We are thriving in love. We are love. We are joyous. We are victorious. We are prosperous. We are peaceful. We are harmonious. It is done and so. *Amen.*

a new life watered [in Love]

Poet C. Nzingha Smith

Parched

brittle

unlubricated bones

cemented in the agony of

alleged loneliness

rub up against

the thought of since-lived experiences,

memories created in love.

The oil of youth

poured out from

mercy's reserves

seeps

between   inflexible   heartstrings

of resentment and bitterness

recalling

abandon in love.

Childhood laughter

transparency

original intent

echoes lightheartedly

against

the gonging of false expectations

remembering

agility in love.

Friction between the new and old me

causes wrong perception to

loosen its hold,

sensation returns

creating a spark

quiet passion

since   forgotten

reawakened in love.

Acceptance

heals

recovers

frees

suppressed emotions

absent of

unfair judgment and unnecessary

restraints in love.

Unrestricted

mindful

not to be stifled   again and again

by the elements

outside of one's control

before, dying to be tended to

now, invigorated and nourished

coming back to authenticity

life, resurrected from its own ability

to water itself

in love.

Author Disclaimer

The stories, characters, and scenarios used as examples throughout the book are based off real situations but have been fictionalized to protect the identities of my clients.

Any names or likeness to actual persons, either living or dead, is strictly coincidental. This book is designed to provide information and motivation to readers. Neither the publisher nor author shall be liable for any physical, psychological, emotional, financial, or commercial damages, including, but not limited to, special, incidental, consequential or other damages.

Every person is different and the advice and strategies contained herein may not be suitable for your situation. Our views and rights are the same: You are responsible for your own choices, actions, and results.

About the Author

———⫸⫷———

Stephan Labossiere is *the* "Relationship Guy." An authority on real love, real talk, real relationships. The brand Stephan Speaks is synonymous with happier relationships and healthier people around the globe. For more than a decade, Stephan has committed himself to breaking down relationship barriers, pushing past common facades, and exposing the truth. It is his understanding of REAL relationships that has empowered millions of people, clients and readers alike, to create their best lives by being able to experience and sustain greater love.

Seen, heard, and chronicled in national and international media outlets including; the *Tom Joyner Morning Show*, *The Examiner*, *ABC*, *GQ*, and *Huffington Post Live*. The certified life & relationship coach, speaker, and award winning, bestselling author is the voice that the world tunes into for answers to their difficult relationship woes. From understanding the opposite sex, to navigating the paths and avoiding the pitfalls of relationships and self-growth, Stephan's relationship advice and insight helps countless men and women overcome the situations hindering them from achieving an authentically amazing life.

Stephan is highly sought-after because he is able to dispel the myths of relationship breakdowns and obstacles–platonic, romantic, and otherwise—with fervor and finesse. His signature style, relatability, and passion make international audiences sit up and pay attention.

"My message is simple: life and relationships require truth. The willingness to speak truth and the bravery to acknowledge truth is paramount."

Are you listening?

Enough said.

COMING SOON BY
Stephan Speaks

www.AffirmationsForHealing.com

JUST RELEASED BY
Stephan Speaks

www.LoveAfterHeartbreak.com

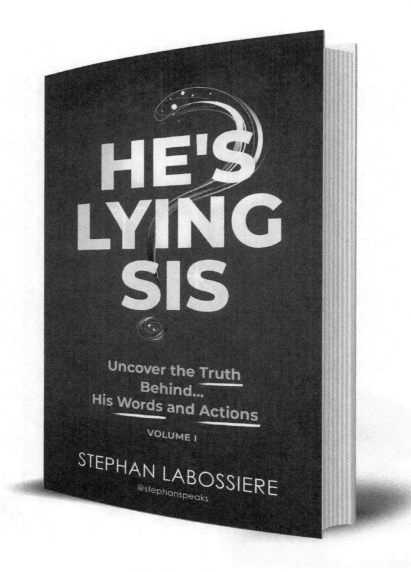

www.HesLyingSis.com

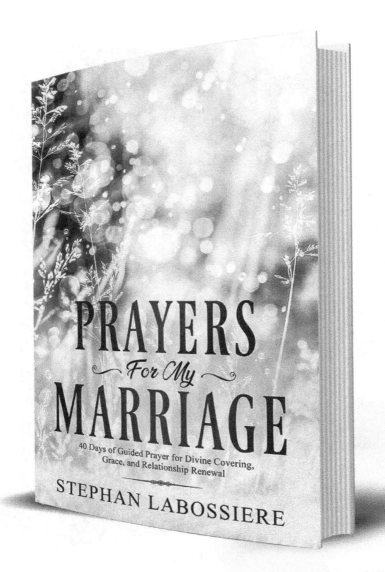

www.PrayersForMyMarriageBook.com

POPULAR BOOKS BY
Stephan Speaks

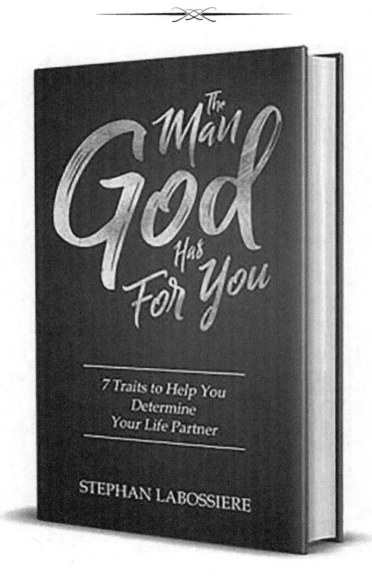

www.TheManGodHasForMe.com

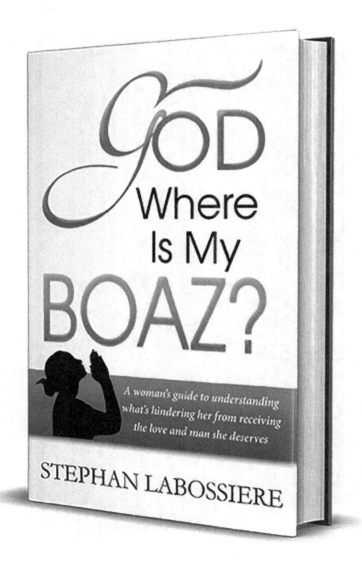

www.GodWhereIsMyBoaz.com

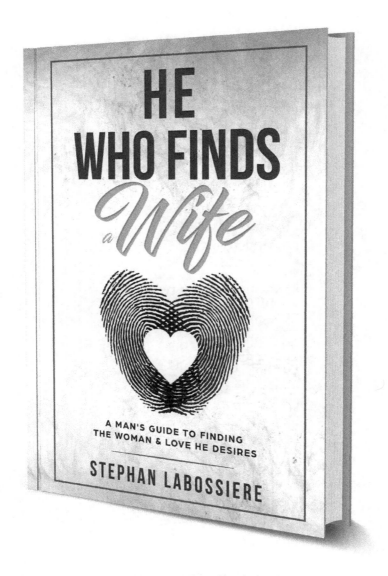

www.HeWhoFinds.com

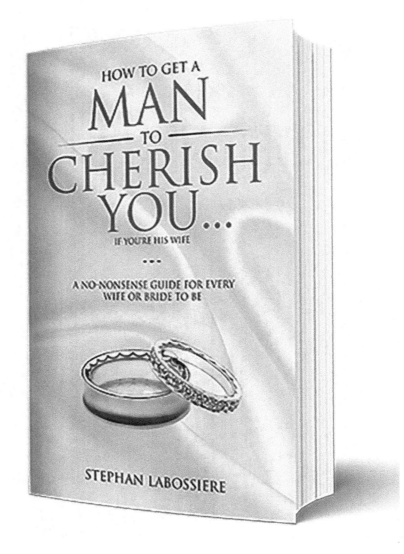

www.GetAManToCherishYou.com

www.BetterMarriageBetterLoving.com

WHAT CLIENTS & READERS
ARE SAYING ABOUT
Stephan Speaks

INSIGHT & HONESTY

Stephan Labossiere has a rare blend of compassion, insight and honesty. He understands relationships, and is a supportive partner and guide on your journey to creating the love and life you want.

—Lisa Marie Bobby

HE'S FUN & LOVING

You hear people saying you must love yourself first, so you can attract the love of your life. This is what I wanted, and for me I did not quite know what this meant until I worked with Stephan. His work is fun, he is very loving, and you get results fast, because he sees very clearly what is going on. I truly recommend signing up for his coaching!

—Dominique, *Paris, France*

A JOY TO WORK WITH

As someone who has studied the role of men and women in relationships in our society for many years, it has been a joy to get to know and work with Stephan. His knowledge and candid from the heart writings and speaking on the topic of relationships are a breath of fresh air and sure to take you and your relationships to a more authentic and loving way of being.

—Tom Preston

More relationship resources can be found at
www.StephanSpeaks.com/shop/

You can also follow me on
Twitter & Instagram: @StephanSpeaks
or find me on Facebook under
"Stephan Speaks Relationships"